Pictures of the Floating World

Pictures of the Floating World

Amy Lowell

MINT EDITIONS

Pictures of the Floating World was first published in 1919.

This edition published by Mint Editions 2023.

ISBN 9798888970041 | E-ISBN 9798888970195

Published by Mint Editions®

 MINT
EDITIONS

minteditionbooks.com

Publishing Director: Katie Connolly
Design: Ponderosa Pine Design
Production and Project Management: Micaela Clark
Typesetting: Westchester Publishing Services

"In the name of these States and in your and my name, the Past,
And in the name of these States and in your and my name, the Present time."

—Walt Whitman. "WITH ANTECEDENTS."

Contents

PLUMMETS TO CIRCUMSTANCE

AS TOWARD WAR

FOREWORD

The march of peoples is always toward the West, wherefore, the earth being round, in time the West must be East again. A startling paradox, but one which accounts for the great interest and inspiration that both poets and painters are discovering in Oriental art. The first part of this book represents some of the charm I have found in delving into Chinese and Japanese poetry. It should be understood, however, that these poems, written in a quasi-Oriental idiom, are not translations except in a very few instances all of which have been duly acknowledged in the text.

In the Japanese "Lacquer Prints," the *hokku* pattern has been more closely followed than has any corresponding Chinese form in the "Chinoiseries"; but, even here, I have made no attempt to observe the syllabic rules which are an integral part of all Japanese poetry. I have endeavoured only to keep the brevity and suggestion of the *hokku*, and to preserve it within its natural sphere. Some of the subjects are purely imaginary, some are taken from legends or historical events, others owe their inception to the vivid, realistic colour-prints of the Japanese masters, but all alike are peculiar to one corner of the globe and, for the most part, to one epoch—the eighteenth century.

The second half of the volume, "Planes of Personality," consists of lyrical poems, deriving from everywhere and nowhere as is the case with all poetry, and needing no introduction. They have been written at various times during the last five years—the earliest, immediately after the publication of *Sword Blades and Poppy Seed*; the most recent, only yesterday. They are here collected for the first time, since the scheme of my last two books of poetry, Men, *Women and Ghosts* and *Can Grande's Castle*, necessarily forbade their inclusion in those volumes.

Amy Lowell

Brookline, Mass.
April 27, 1919

LACQUER PRINTS

LACQUER PRINTS
(Adapted from the poet Yakura Sanjin, 1769)

As I wandered through the eight hundred and eight streets of the city,
I saw nothing so beautiful
As the Women of the Green Houses,
With their girdles of spun gold,
And their long-sleeved dresses,
Coloured like the graining of wood.
As they walk,
The hems of their outer garments flutter open,
And the blood-red linings glow like sharp-toothed maple leaves
In Autumn.

By Messenger

One night
When there was a clear moon,
I sat down
To write a poem
About maple-trees.
But the dazzle of moonlight
In the ink
Blinded me,
And I could only write
What I remembered.
Therefore, on the wrapping of my poem
I have inscribed your name.

Circumstance

Upon the maple leaves
The dew shines red,
But on the lotus blossom
It has the pale transparence of tears.

Angles

The rain is dark against the white sky,
Or white against the foliage of eucalyptus-trees.
But, in the cistern, it is a sheet of mauve and amber,
Because of the chrysanthemums
Heaped about its edge.

Vicarious

When I stand under the willow-tree
Above the river,
In my straw-coloured silken garment
Embroidered with purple chrysanthemums,
It is not at the bright water
That I am gazing,
But at your portrait,
Which I have caused to be painted
On my fan.

Near Kioto

I crossed over the bridge of Ariwarano Narikira,
I saw that the waters were purple
With the floating leaves of maples.

AMY LOWELL

DESOLATION

Under the plum-blossoms are nightingales;
But the sea is hidden in an egg-white mist,
And they are silent.

Yoshiwara Lament

Golden peacocks
Under blossoming cherry-trees,
But on all the wide sea
There is no boat.

Sunshine

The pool is edged with the blade-like leaves of irises.
If I throw a stone into the placid water,
It suddenly stiffens
Into rings and rings
Of sharp gold wire.

Illusion

Walking beside the tree-peonies,
I saw a beetle
Whose wings were of black lacquer spotted with milk.
I would have caught it,
But it ran from me swiftly
And hid under the stone lotus
Which supports the statue of Buddha.

A Year Passes

Beyond the porcelain fence of the pleasure garden,
I hear the frogs in the blue-green rice-fields;
But the sword-shaped moon
Has cut my heart in two.

A Lover

If I could catch the green lantern of the firefly
I could see to write you a letter.

To a Husband

Brighter than fireflies upon the Uji River
Are your words in the dark, Beloved.

The Fisherman's Wife

When I am alone,
The wind in the pine-trees
Is like the shuffling of waves
Upon the wooden sides of a boat.

FROM CHINA

I thought:—
The moon,
Shining upon the many steps of the palace before me,
Shines also upon the chequered rice-fields
Of my native land.
And my tears fell
Like white rice grains
At my feet.

The Pond

Cold, wet leaves
Floating on moss-coloured water,
And the croaking of frogs—
Cracked bell-notes in the twilight.

Autumn

All day I have watched the purple vine leaves
Fall into the water.
And now in the moonlight they still fall,
But each leaf is fringed with silver.

Ephemera

Silver-green lanterns tossing among windy branches:
So an old man thinks
Of the loves of his youth.

AMY LOWELL

Document

The great painter, Hokusai,
In his old age,
Wrote these words:
  "Profiting by a beautiful Spring day,
  In this year of tranquillity,
  To warm myself in the sun,
  I received a visit from my publisher
  Who asked me to do something for him.
  Then I reflected that one should not forget the glory of arms,
  Above all when one was living in peace;
  And in spite of my age,
  Which is more than seventy years,
  I have found courage to draw those ancient heroes
  Who have been the models of glory."

The Emperor's Garden

Once, in the sultry heats of Midsummer,
An Emperor caused the miniature mountains in his garden

To be covered with white silk,
That so crowned
They might cool his eyes
With the sparkle of snow.

One of the "Hundred Views of Fuji" by Hokusai

Being thirsty,
I filled a cup with water,
And, behold!
Fuji-yama lay upon the water
Like a dropped leaf!

Disillusion

A scholar,
Weary of erecting the fragile towers of words,
Went on a pilgrimage to Asama-yama.
And seeing the force of the fire
Spouting from this mighty mountain,
Hurled himself into its crater
And perished.

Paper Fishes

The paper carp,
At the end of its long bamboo pole,
Takes the wind into its mouth
And emits it at its tail.
So is man,
Forever swallowing the wind.

MEDITATION

A wise man,
Watching the stars pass across the sky,
Remarked:
In the upper air the fireflies move more slowly.

THE CAMELLIA TREE OF MATSUE

At Matsue,
There was a Camellia Tree of great beauty
Whose blossoms were white as honey wax
Splashed and streaked with the pink of fair coral.
At night,
When the moon rose in the sky,
The Camellia Tree would leave its place
By the gateway,
And wander up and down the garden,
Trailing its roots behind it
Like a train of rustling silk.
The people in the house,
Hearing the scrape of them upon the gravel,
Looked out into the garden
And saw the tree,
With its flowers erect and peering,
Pressed against the shoji.
Many nights the tree walked about the garden,
Until the women and children
Became frightened,
And the Master of the house
Ordered that it be cut down.
But when the gardener brought his axe
And struck at the trunk of the tree,
There spouted forth a stream of dark blood;
And when the stump was torn up,
The hole quivered like an open wound.

Superstition

I have painted a picture of a ghost
Upon my kite,
And hung it on a tree.
Later, when I loose the string
And let it fly,
The people will cower
And hide their heads,
For fear of the God
Swimming in the clouds.

AMY LOWELL

THE RETURN

Coming up from my boat
In haste to lighten your anxiety,
I saw, reflected in the circular metal mirror,
The face and hands of a woman
Arranging her hair.

A Lady to Her Lover

The white snows of Winter
Follow the falling of leaves;
Therefore
I have had your portrait cut
In snow-white jade.

Nuance

Even the iris bends
When a butterfly lights upon it.

Autumn Haze

Is it a dragonfly or a maple leaf
That settles softly down upon the water?

Peace

Perched upon the muzzle of a cannon
A yellow butterfly is slowly opening and shutting its wings.

In Time of War

Across the newly-plastered wall,
The darting of red dragonflies
Is like the shooting Of blood-tipped arrows.

Nuit Blanche

The chirping of crickets in the night
Is intermittent,
Like the twinkling of stars.

SPRING DAWN

He wore a coat
With gold and red maple leaves,
He was girt with the two swords,
He carried a peony lantern.
When I awoke,
There was only the blue shadow of the plum-tree
Upon the shoji.

POETRY

Over the shop where silk is sold
Still the dragon kites are flying.

From a Window

Your footfalls on the drum bridge beside my house
Are like the pattering drops of a passing shower,
So soon are they gone.

Again the New Year Festival

I have drunk your health
In the red-lacquer wine cups,
But the wind-bells on the bronze lanterns
In my garden
Are corroded and fallen.

TIME

Looking at myself in my metal mirror,
I saw, faintly outlined,
The figure of a crane
Engraved upon its back.

Legend

When the leaves of the cassia-tree
Turn red in Autumn,
Then the moon,
In which it grows,
Shines for many nights
More brightly

Pilgrims Ascending Fuji-Yama

I should tremble at the falling showers of ashes
Dislodged by my feet,
Did I not know
That at night they fly upward
And spread themselves once more
Upon the slopes of the Honourable Mountain.

The Kagoes of a Returning Traveller

Diagonally between the cryptomerias,
What I took for the flapping of wings
Was the beating feet of your runners,
O my Lord!

A Street

Under red umbrellas with cream-white centres,
A procession of Geisha passes
In front of the silk-shop of Matsuzaka-ya.

Outside a Gate

On the floor of the empty palanquin
The plum-petals constantly increase.

Road to the Yoshiwara

Coming to you along the Nihon Embankment,
Suddenly the road was darkened
By a flock of wild geese
Crossing the moon.

AMY LOWELL

Ox Street, Takanawa

What is a rainbow?
Have I not seen its colours and its shape
Duplicated in the melon slices
Lying beside an empty cart?

A Daimio's Oiran

When I hear your runners shouting:
"Get down! Get down!"
Then I dress my hair
With the little chrysanthemums.

Passing the Bamboo Fence

What fell upon my open umbrella—
A plum-blossom?

Frosty Evening

It is not the bright light in your window
Which dazzles my eyes;
It is the dim outline of your shadow
Moving upon the shōji.

An Artist

The anchorite, Kisen,
Composed a thousand poems
And threw nine hundred and ninety-nine into the river
Finding one alone worthy of preservation.

A Burnt Offering

Because there was no wind,
The smoke of your letters hung in the air
For a long time;
And its shape
Was the shape of your face,
My Beloved.

Daybreak, Yoshiwara

Draw your hoods tightly,
You who must depart,
The morning mist
Is grey and miasmic.

Temple Ceremony
(From the Japanese of Sōjo Henjō)

Blow softly,
O Wind!
And let no clouds cover the moon
Which lights the posturing steps
Of the most beautiful of dancers.

Two Porters Returning Along a Country Road

Since an empty kago can be carried upon the back of one man,
Therefore the other has nothing to do
But gaze at the white circle
Drawn about the flying moon.

Storm by the Seashore

There is no moon in the sky,
But with each step
I see one grow in the sand
Under my feet.
This interests me so much
That I forget the rain
Beating against the lantern
Which my cloak only partially covers.

The Exiled Emperor

The birds sing today,
For tomorrow they will be flown
Many miles across the tossing sea.

Letter Written from Prison by two Political Offenders

When a hero fails of his purpose,
His acts are regarded as those of a villain and a robber.
Pursuing liberty, suddenly our plans are defeated.
In public we have been seized and pinioned and caged for many days.
How can we find exit from this place?
Weeping, we seem as fools; laughing, as rogues.
Alas! for us; we can only be silent.

Moon Haze

Because the moonlight deceives
Therefore I love it.

Proportion

In the sky there is a moon and stars,
And in my garden there are yellow moths
Fluttering about a white azalea bush.

CONSTANCY

Although so many years,
Still the vows we made each other
Remain tied to the great trunk
Of the seven separate trees
In the courtyard of the Crimson Temple
At Nara.

CHINOISERIES

REFLECTIONS

When I looked into your eyes,
I saw a garden
With peonies, and tinkling pagodas,
And round-arched bridges
Over still lakes.
A woman sat beside the water
In a rain-blue, silken garment.
She reached through the water
To pluck the crimson peonies
Beneath the surface,
But as she grasped the stems,
They jarred and broke into white-green ripples;
And as she drew out her hand,
The water-drops dripping from it
Stained her rain-blue dress like tears.

Falling Snow

The snow whispers about me,
And my wooden clogs
Leave holes behind me in the snow.
But no one will pass this way
Seeking my footsteps,
And when the temple bell rings again
They will be covered and gone.

AMY LOWELL

Hoar-Frost

In the cloud-grey mornings
I heard the herons flying;
And when I came into my garden,
My silken outer-garment
Trailed over withered leaves.
A dried leaf crumbles at a touch,
But I have seen many Autumns
With herons blowing like smoke
Across the sky.

GOLD-LEAF SCREEN

Under the broken clouds of dawn,
The white leopards eat the grapes
In my vineyard.
And in the sunken splendour of twilight,
The ring pheasants perch among the red fruit
Of my pomegranate trees.
The bright coloured varnish
Scales off the wheels of my chariots,
For the horses which should draw them
Have gone Northward in a gloom of spears.
My stablemen march,
Each with a two-edged spear upon his shoulder,
And my orchard tenders have put on the green feathered helmets
And girt themselves with black bows.
I stand above the terrace of three hundred rose-trees
And gaze at my despoiled vineyards.
Drums beat among the Northern hills,
But I hear only the rattle of the wind on the chipped tiles
Of my roof.

A thousand little stitches in the soul of a dead man—
Still one can enjoy these things
Sitting over a fire of camphor wood
In a quilted gown of purple-red silk.

A POET'S WIFE
Cho Wen-chiin to her husband Ssu-ma Hsiang-ju

You have taken our love and turned it into coins of silver.
You sell the love poems you wrote for me,
And with the price of them you buy many cups of wine.
I beg that you remain dumb,
That you write no more poems.
For the wine does us both an injury,
And the words of your heart
Have become the common speech of the Emperor's concubines.

SPRING LONGING

The South wind blows open the folds of my dress,
My feet leave wet tracks in the earth of my garden,
The willows along the canal sing with new leaves turned upon the wind.
   I walk along the tow-path
   Gazing at the level water.
   Should I see a ribbed edge
   Running upon its clearness,
   I should know that this was caused
   By the prow of the boat
   In which you are to return.

Li T'ai Po

So, Master, the wine gave you something,
I suppose.

I think I see you,
Your silks all disarranged,
Lolling in a green-marble pavilion,
Ogling the concubines of the Emperor's Court
Who pass the door
In yellow coats, and white jade ear-drops,
Their hair pleated in folds like the hundred clouds.
I watch you,
Hiccoughing poetry between drinks,
Sinking as the sun sinks,
Sleeping for twenty-four hours,
While they peek at you,
Giggling,
Through the open door.

You found something in the wine,
I imagine,
Since you could not leave it,
Even when, after years of wandering,
You sat in the boat with one sail,
Travelling down the zigzag rivers
On your way back to Court.

You had a dream,
I conjecture.
You saw something under the willow-lights of the water
Which swept you to dizziness,
So that you toppled over the edge of the boat,
And gasped, and became your dream.
Twelve hundred years
Or thereabouts.
Did the wine do it?
I would sit in the purple moonlight

And drink three hundred cups,
If I believed it.
Three hundred full cups,
After your excellent fashion,
While in front of me
The river dazzle ran before the moon,
And the light flaws of the evening wind
Scattered the notes of nightingales
Loosely among the kuai trees.

They erected a temple to you:
"Great Doctor,
Prince of Poetry,
Immortal man who loved drink."
I detest wine,
And I have no desire for the temple,
Which under the circumstances
Is fortunate.
But I would sacrifice even sobriety
If, when I was thoroughly drunk,
I could see what you saw
Under the willow-clouded water,
The day you died.

PLANES OF PERSONALITY

TWO SPEAK TOGETHER

VERNAL EQUINOX

The scent of hyacinths, like a pale mist, lies between me and my book;
And the South Wind, washing through the room,
Makes the candles quiver.
My nerves sting at a spatter of rain on the shutter,
And I am uneasy with the thrusting of green shoots
Outside, in the night.

Why are you not here to overpower me with your tense and urgent love?

The Letter

Little cramped words scrawling all over the paper
Like draggled fly's legs,
What can you tell of the flaring moon
Through the oak leaves?
Or of my uncurtained window and the bare floor
Spattered with moonlight?
Your silly quirks and twists have nothing in them
Of blossoming hawthorns,
And this paper is dull, crisp, smooth, virgin of loveliness
Beneath my hand.

I am tired, Beloved, of chafing my heart against
The want of you;
Of squeezing it into little inkdrops,
And posting it.
And I scald alone, here, under the fire
Of the great moon.

AMY LOWELL

Mise En Scène

When I think of you, Beloved,
I see a smooth and stately garden
With parterres of gold and crimson tulips
And bursting lilac leaves.
There is a low-lipped basin in the midst,
Where a statue of veined cream marble
Perpetually pours water over her shoulder
From a rounded urn.
When the wind blows,
The water-stream blows before it
And spatters into the basin with a light tinkling,
And your shawl—the colour of red violets
Flares out behind you in great curves
Like the swirling draperies of a painted Madonna.

Venus Transiens

Tell me,
Was Venus more beautiful
Than you are,
When she topped
The crinkled waves,
Drifting shoreward
On her plaited shell?
Was Botticelli's vision
Fairer than mine;
And were the painted rosebuds
He tossed his lady,
Of better worth
Than the words I blow about you
To cover your too great loveliness
As with a gauze
Of misted silver?
For me,
You stand poised
In the blue and buoyant air,
Cinctured by bright winds,
Treading the sunlight.
And the waves which precede you
Ripple and stir
The sands at my feet.

AMY LOWELL

MADONNA OF THE EVENING FLOWERS

All day long I have been working,
Now I am tired.
I call: "Where are you?"
But there is only the oak-tree rustling in the wind.
The house is very quiet,
The sun shines in on your books,
On your scissors and thimble just put down,
But you are not there.
Suddenly I am lonely:
Where are you?
I go about searching.

Then I see you,
Standing under a spire of pale blue larkspur,
With a basket of roses on your arm.
You are cool, like silver,
And you smile.
I think the Canterbury bells are playing little tunes.

You tell me that the peonies need spraying,
That the columbines have overrun all bounds,
That the pyrus japonica should be cut back and rounded.
You tell me these things.
But I look at you, heart of silver,
White heart-flame of polished silver,
Burning beneath the blue steeples of the larkspur,
And I long to kneel instantly at your feet,
While all about us peal the loud, sweet *Te Deums* of the Canterbury bells.

Bright Sunlight

The wind has blown a corner of your shawl
Into the fountain,
Where it floats and drifts
Among the lily-pads
Like a tissue of sapphires.
But you do not heed it,
Your fingers pick at the lichens
On the stone edge of the basin,
And your eyes follow the tall clouds
As they sail over the ilex-trees

OMBRE CHINOISE

Red foxgloves against a yellow wall streaked with plum-coloured shadows;
A lady with a blue and red sunshade;
The slow dash of waves upon a parapet.
That is all.
Non-existent—immortal—
As solid as the centre of a ring of fine gold.

JULY MIDNIGHT

Fireflies flicker in the tops of trees,
Flicker in the lower branches,
Skim along the ground.
Over the moon-white lilies
Is a flashing and ceasing of small, lemon-green stars.
As you lean against me,
Moon-white,
The air all about you
Is slit, and pricked, and pointed with sparkles of lemon-green flame
Starting out of a background of vague, blue trees.

WHEAT-IN-THE-EAR

You stand between the cedars and the green spruces,
Brilliantly naked.
And I think:
    What are you,
    A gem under sunlight?
    A poised spear?
    A jade cup?
You flash in front of the cedars and the tall spruces,
And I see that you are fire
Sacrificial fire on a jade altar,
Spear-tongue of white, ceremonial fire.
My eyes burn,
My hands are flames seeking you,
But you are as remote from me as a bright pointed planet
Set in the distance of an evening sky.

The Weather-Cock Points South

I put your leaves aside,
One by one:
The stiff, broad outer leaves;
The smaller ones,
Pleasant to touch, veined with purple;
The glazed inner leaves.
One by one
I parted you from your leaves,
Until you stood up like a white flower
Swaying slightly in the evening wind.

White flower,
Flower of wax, of jade, of unstreaked agate;
Flower with surfaces of ice,
With shadows faintly crimson.
Where in all the garden is there such a flower?
The stars crowd through the lilac leaves
To look at you.
The low moon brightens you with silver.

The bud is more than the calyx.
There is nothing to equal a white bud,
Of no colour, and of all,
Burnished by moonlight,
Thrust upon by a softly-swinging wind.

The Artist

Why do you subdue yourself in golds and purples?
Why do you dim yourself with folded silks?
Do you not see that I can buy brocades in any draper's shop,
And that I am choked in the twilight of all these colours.
How pale you would be, and startling,
How quiet;
But your curves would spring upward
Like a clear jet of flung water,
You would quiver like a shot-up spray of water,
You would waver, and relapse, and tremble.
And I too should tremble,
Watching.

Murex-dyes and tinsel—
And yet I think I could bear your beauty unshaded.

THE GARDEN BY MOONLIGHT

A black cat among roses,
Phlox, lilac-misted under a first-quarter moon,
The sweet smells of heliotrope and night-scented stock.
The garden is very still,
It is dazed with moonlight,
Contented with perfume,
Dreaming the opium dreams of its folded poppies.
Firefly lights open and vanish
High as the tip buds of the golden glow
Low as the sweet alyssum flowers at my feet.
Moon-shimmer on leaves and trellises,
Moon-spikes shafting through the snow-ball bush.
Only the little faces of the ladies' delight are alert and staring,
Only the cat, padding between the roses,
Shakes a branch and breaks the chequered pattern
As water is broken by the falling of a leaf.
Then you come,
And you are quiet like the garden,
And white like the alyssum flowers,
And beautiful as the silent sparks of the fireflies.
Ah, Beloved, do you see those orange lilies?
They knew my mother,
But who belonging to me will they know
When I am gone.

AMY LOWELL

INTERLUDE

When I have baked white cakes
And grated green almonds to spread upon them;
When I have picked the green crowns from the strawberries
And piled them, cone-pointed, in a blue and yellow platter;
When I have smoothed the seam of the linen I have been working;
What then?
Tomorrow it will be the same:
Cakes and strawberries,
And needles in and out of cloth.
If the sun is beautiful on bricks and pewter,
How much more beautiful is the moon,
Slanting down the gauffered branches of a plum-tree;
The moon,
Wavering across a bed of tulips;
The moon,
Still,
Upon your face.
You shine, Beloved,
You and the moon.
But which is the reflection?
The clock is striking eleven.
I think, when we have shut and barred the door,
The night will be dark
Outside.

Bullion

My thoughts
Chink against my ribs
And roll about like silver hail-stones.
I should like to spill them out,
And pour them, all shining,
Over you.
But my heart is shut upon them
And holds them straitly.

Come, You! and open my heart;
That my thoughts torment me no longer,
But glitter in your hair.

The Wheel of the Sun

I beg you
Hide your face from me.
Draw the tissue of your head-gear
Over your eyes.
For I am blinded by your beauty,
And my heart is strained,
And aches,
Before you.

In the street,
You spread a brightness where you walk,
And I see your lifting silks
And rejoice;
But I cannot look up to your face.
You melt my strength,
And set my knees to trembling.
Shadow yourself that I may love you,
For now it is too great a pain.

A Shower

That sputter of rain, flipping the hedge-rows
And making the highways hiss,
How I love it!
And the touch of you upon my arm
As you press against me that my umbrella
May cover you.

Tinkle of drops on stretched silk.
Wet murmur through green branches.

Summer Rain

All night our room was outer-walled with rain.
Drops fell and flattened on the tin roof,
And rang like little disks of metal.
Ping!—Ping!—and there was not a pin-point of silence between them.
The rain rattled and clashed,
And the slats of the shutters danced and glittered.
But to me the darkness was red-gold and crocus coloured
With your brightness,
And the words you whispered to me
Sprang up and flamed—orange torches against the rain.
Torches against the wall of cool, silver rain!

April

A bird chirped at my window this morning,
And over the sky is drawn a light network of clouds. Come,
Let us go out into the open,
For my heart leaps like a fish that is ready to spawn.

I will lie under the beech-trees,
Under the grey branches of the beech-trees,
In a blueness of little squills and crocuses.
I will lie among the little squills
And be delivered of this overcharge of beauty,
And that which is born shall be a joy to you
Who love me.

Coq D'or

I walked along a street at dawn in cold, grey light,
Above me lines of windows watched, gaunt, dull, drear.
The lamps were fading, and the sky was streaked rose-red,
Silhouetting chimneys with their queer, round pots.
My feet upon the pavement made a knock—knock—knock.
Above the roofs of Westminster, Big Ben struck.
The cocks on all the steeples crew in clear, flat tones,
And churchyard daisies sprang away from thin, bleak bones.
The golden trees were calling me: "Come! Come! Come!"
The trees were fresh with daylight, and I heard bees hum.
A cart trailed slowly down the street, its load young greens,
They sparkled like blown emeralds, and then I laughed.
A morning in the city with its upthrust spires
All tipped with gold and shining in the brisk, blue air,
But the gold is round my forehead and the knot still holds
Where you tied it in the shadows, your rose-gold hair.

THE CHARM

I lay them before you,
One, two, three silver pieces,
And a copper piece
Dulled with handling.
The first will buy you a cake,
The second a flower,
The third a coloured bead.
The fourth will buy you nothing at all,
Since it has a hole in it.
I beg you, therefore,
String it about your neck,
At least it will remind you of my poverty.

After a Storm

You walk under the ice trees.
They sway, and crackle,
And arch themselves splendidly
To deck your going.
The white sun flips them into colour
Before you.
They are blue,
And mauve,
And emerald.
They are amber,
And jade,
And sardonyx.
They are silver fretted to flame
And startled to stillness,
Bunched, splintered, iridescent.
You walk under the ice trees
And the bright snow creaks as you step upon it.
My dogs leap about you,
And their barking strikes upon the air
Like sharp hammer-strokes on metal.
You walk under the ice trees
But you are more dazzling than the ice flowers,
And the dogs' barking
Is not so loud to me as your quietness.

You walk under the ice trees
At ten o'clock in the morning.

Opal

You are ice and fire,
The touch of you burns my hands like snow.
You are cold and flame.
You are the crimson of amaryllis,
The silver of moon-touched magnolias.
When I am with you,
My heart is a frozen pond
Gleaming with agitated torches.

Wakefulness

Jolt of market-carts;
Steady drip of horses' hoofs on hard pavement;
A black sky lacquered over with blueness,
And the lights of Battersea Bridge
Pricking pale in the dawn.
The beautiful hours are passing
And still you sleep!
Tired heart of my joy,
Incurved upon your dreams,
Will the day come before you have opened to me?

Orange of Midsummer

You came to me in the pale starting of Spring,
And I could not see the world
For the blue mist of wonder before my eyes.
You beckoned me over a rainbow bridge,
And I set foot upon it, trembling.
Through pearl and saffron I followed you,
Through heliotrope and rose,
Iridescence after iridescence,
And to me it was all one
Because of the blue mist that held my eyes.

You came again, and it was red-hearted Summer.
You called to me across a field of poppies and wheat,
With a narrow path slicing through it
Straight to an outer boundary of trees.
And I ran along the path,
Brushing over the yellow wheat beside it,
And came upon you under a maple-tree, plaiting poppies for a girdle.
"Are you thirsty?" said you,
And held out a cup.
But the water in the cup was scarlet and crimson
Like the poppies in your hands.
"It looks like blood," I said.
"Like blood," you said,
"Does it?
But drink it, my Beloved."

SHORE GRASS

The moon is cold over the sand-dunes,
And the clumps of sea-grasses flow and glitter;
The thin chime of my watch tells the quarter after midnight;
And still I hear nothing
But the windy beating of the sea.

Autumnal Equinox

Why do you not sleep, Beloved?

It is so cold that the stars stand out of the sky
Like golden nails not driven home.
The fire crackles pleasantly,
And I sit here listening
For your regular breathing from the room above.

What keeps you awake, Beloved?
Is it the same nightmare that keeps me strained with listening
So that I cannot read?

AMY LOWELL

The Country House

Did the door move, or was it always ajar?
The gladioli on the table are pale mauve.
I smell pale mauve and blue,
Blue soft like bruises—putrid—oozing—
The air oozes blue—mauve—
And the door with the black line where it does not shut!

I must pass that door to go to bed,
Or I must stay here
And watch the crack
Oozing air.

Is it—air?

NERVES

The lake is steel-coloured and umber,
And a clutter of gaunt clouds blows rapidly across the sky.

I wonder why you chose to be buried
In this little grave-yard by the lake-side.
It is all very well on blue mornings,
Summer mornings,
Autumn mornings polished with sunlight.
But in Winter, in the cold storms,
When there is no wind,
And the snow murmurs as it falls!
The grave-stones glimmer in the twilight
As though they were rubbed with phosphorous.
The direct road is up a hill,
Through woods—
I will take the lake road,
I can drive faster there.
You used to like to drive with me
Why does death make you this fearful thing?
Flick!—flack!—my horse's feet strike the stones.
There is a house just round the bend.

AMY LOWELL

LEFT BEHIND

White phlox and white hydrangeas,
High, thin clouds,
A low, warm sun.
So it is this afternoon.
But the phlox will be a drift of petals,
And the hydrangeas stained and fallen
Before you come again.
I cannot look at the flowers,
Nor the lifting leaves of the trees.
Without you, there is no garden,
No bright colours,
No shining leaves.
There is only space,
Stretching endlessly forward—
And I walk, bent, unseeing,
Waiting to catch the first faint scuffle
Of withered leaves.

Autumn

They brought me a quilled, yellow dahlia,
Opulent, flaunting.
Round gold
Flung out of a pale green stalk.
Round, ripe gold
Of maturity,
Meticulously frilled and flaming,
A fire-ball of proclamation:
Fecundity decked in staring yellow
For all the world to see.
They brought a quilled, yellow dahlia,
To me who am barren.
Shall I send it to you,
You who have taken with you
All I once possessed?

The Sixteenth Floor

The noise of the city sounds below me.
It clashes against the houses
And rises like smoke through the narrow streets.
It polishes the marble fronts of houses,
Grating itself against them,
And they shine in the lamplight
And cast their echoes back upon the asphalt of the streets.

But I hear no sound of your voice,
The city is incoherent—trivial,
And my brain aches with emptiness.

Strain

It is late
And the clock is striking thin hours,
But sleep has become a terror to me,
Lest I wake in the night
Bewildered,
And stretching out my arms to comfort myself with you,
Clasp instead the cold body of the darkness.
All night it will hunger over me,
And push and undulate against me,
Breathing into my mouth
And passing long fingers through my drifting hair.
Only the dawn can loose me from it,
And the grey streaks of morning melt it from my side.

Bring many candles,
Though they stab my tired brain
And hurt it.
For I am afraid of the twining of the darkness
And dare not sleep.

AMY LOWELL

HAUNTED

See! He trails his toes
Through the long streaks of moonlight,
And the nails of his fingers glitter:
They claw and flash among the tree-tops.
His lips suck at my open window,
And his breath creeps about my body
And lies in pools under my knees.
I can see his mouth sway and wobble,
Sticking itself against the window-jambs,
But the moonlight is bright on the floor,
Without a shadow.
Hark! A hare is strangling in the forest,
And the wind tears a shutter from the wall.

GROTESQUE

Why do the lilies goggle their tongues at me
When I pluck them;
And writhe, and twist,
And strangle themselves against my fingers,
So that I can hardly weave the garland
For your hair?
Why do they shriek your name
And spit at me
When I would cluster them?
Must I kill them
To make them lie still,
And send you a wreath of lolling corpses
To turn putrid and soft
On your forehead
While you dance?

Snow in April

Sunshine!
Sunshine!
Smooth blue skies,
Fresh winds through early tree-tops,
Pointed shoots,
White bells,
White and purple cups.
I am a plum-tree
Checked at its flowering.
My blossoms wither,
My branches grow brittle again.
I stretch them out and up,
But the snowflakes fall—
Whirl—and fall.
April and snow,
And my heart stuffed and suffocating.
Dead,
With my blossoms brown and dropping
Upon my cold roots.

A Sprig of Rosemary

I cannot see your face.
When I think of you,
It is your hands which I see.
Your hands
Sewing,
Holding a book,
Resting for a moment on the sill of a window.
My eyes keep always the sight of your hands,
But my heart holds the sound of your voice,
And the soft brightness which is your soul.

AMY LOWELL

Maladie De L'après-Midi

Why does the clanking of a tip-cart
In the road
Make me so sad?
The sound beats the air
With flat blows,
Dull and continued.

Not even the clear sunshine
Through bronze and green oak leaves,
Nor the crimson spindle of a cedar-tree
Hooded with Virginia creeper,
Nor the humming brightness of the air,
Can comfort my melancholy.

The cart goes slowly,
It creeps at a foot-pace,
And the flat blows of sound
Hurt me,
And bring me nearly to weeping.

November

The vine leaves against the brick walls of my house
Are rusty and broken.
Dead leaves gather under the pine-trees,
The brittle boughs of lilac-bushes
Sweep against the stars.
And I sit under a lamp
Trying to write down the emptiness of my heart.
Even the cat will not stay with me,
But prefers the rain
Under the meagre shelter of a cellar window.

AMY LOWELL

Nostalgia

"Through pleasures and palaces"—
Through hotels, and Pullman cars, and steamships. . .

Pink and white camellias floating in a crystal bowl,
The sharp smell of firewood,
The scrape and rustle of a dog stretching himself on a hardwood floor,
And your voice, reading—reading—to the slow ticking of an old brass
    clock. . .

"Tickets, please!"
And I watch the man in front of me
Fumbling in fourteen pockets,
While the conductor balances his ticket-punch
Between his fingers.

PREPARATION

Today I went into a shop where they sell spectacles.

"Sir," said the shopman, "what can I do for you?
Are you far-sighted or near-sighted?"

"Neither the one nor the other," said I.
"I can read the messages passing along the telegraph wires,
And I can see the antennae of a fly
Perched upon the bridge of my nose."

"Rose-coloured spectacles, perhaps?" suggested the shopman.

"Indeed, no," said I.
"Were I to add them to my natural vision
I should see everything ruined with blood."

"Green spectacles," opined the shopman.

"By no means," said I.
"I am far too prone to that colour at moments.
No. You can give me some smoked glasses
For I have to meet a train this afternoon."

"What a world yours must be, Sir,"
Observed the shopman as he wrapped up the spectacles,
"When it requires to be dimmed by smoked glasses."

"Not a world," said I, and laid the money down on the counter,
"Certainly not a world.
Good-day."

AMY LOWELL

A DECADE

When you came, you were like red wine and honey,
And the taste of you burnt my mouth with its sweetness.
Now you are like morning bread,
Smooth and pleasant.
I hardly taste you at all for I know your savour,
But I am completely nourished.

PENUMBRA

As I sit here in the quiet Summer night,
Suddenly, from the distant road, there comes
The grind and rush of an electric car.
And, from still farther off,
An engine puffs sharply,
Followed by the drawn-out shunting scrape of a freight train.
These are the sounds that men make
In the long business of living.
They will always make such sounds,
Years after I am dead and cannot hear them.

Sitting here in the Summer night,
I think of my death.
What will it be like for you then?
You will see my chair
With its bright chintz covering
Standing in the afternoon sunshine,
As now.
You will see my narrow table
At which I have written so many hours.
My dogs will push their noses into your hand,
And ask—ask—
Clinging to you with puzzled eyes.

The old house will still be here,
The old house which has known me since the beginning.
The walls which have watched me while I played:
Soldiers, marbles, paper-dolls,
Which have protected me and my books.

The front-door will gaze down among the old trees
Where, as a child, I hunted ghosts and Indians;
It will look out on the wide gravel sweep
Where I rolled my hoop,
And at the rhododendron bushes
Where I caught black-spotted butterflies.

AMY LOWELL

The old house will guard you,
As I have done.
Its walls and rooms will hold you,
And I shall whisper my thoughts and fancies
As always,
From the pages of my books.

You will sit here, some quiet Summer night,
Listening to the puffing trains,
But you will not be lonely,
For these things are a part of me.
And my love will go on speaking to you
Through the chairs, and the tables, and the pictures,
As it does now through my voice,
And the quick, necessary touch of my hand.

Frimaire

Dearest, we are like two flowers
Blooming last in a yellowing garden,
A purple aster flower and a red one
Standing alone in a withered desolation.

The garden plants are shattered and seeded,
One brittle leaf scrapes against another,
Fiddling echoes of a rush of petals.
Now only you and I nodding together.

Many were with us; they have all faded.
Only we are purple and crimson,
Only we in the dew-clear mornings,
Smarten into colour as the sun rises.

When I scarcely see you in the flat moonlight,
And later when my cold roots tighten,
I am anxious for the morning,
I cannot rest in fear of what may happen.

You or I—and I am a coward.
Surely frost should take the crimson.
Purple is a finer colour,
Very splendid in isolation.

So we nod above the broken
Stems of flowers almost rotted.
Many mornings there cannot be now
For us both. Ah, Dear, I love you!

AMY LOWELL

EYES, AND EARS, AND WALKING

Solitaire

When night drifts along the streets of the city,
And sifts down between the uneven roofs,
My mind begins to peek and peer.
It plays at ball in old, blue Chinese gardens,
And shakes wrought dice-cups in Pagan temples
Amid the broken flutings of white pillars.
It dances with purple and yellow crocuses in its hair,
And its feet shine as they flutter over drenched grasses.
How light and laughing my mind is,
When all the good folk have put out their bedroom candles,
And the city is still!

THE BACK BAY FENS
Study in Orange and Silver

Through the Spring-thickened branches
I see it floating,
An ivory dome
Headed to gold by the dim sun.

It hangs against a white-misted sky,
And the swollen branches
Open or cover it,
As they blow in the wet wind.

Free Fantasia on Japanese Themes

All the afternoon there has been a chirping of birds,
And the sun lies, warm and still, on the Western sides of puffed
    branches.
There is no wind,
Even the little twigs at the ends of the branches do not move,
And the needles of the pines are solid,
Bands of inarticulated blackness,
Against the blue-white sky.
Still—but alert—
And my heart is still and alert,
Passive with sunshine
Avid of adventure.

I would experience new emotions—
Submit to strange enchantments—
Bend to influences,
Bizarre, exotic,
Fresh with burgeoning.

I would climb a Sacred Mountain,
Struggle with other pilgrims up a steep path through pine-trees
Above to the smooth, treeless slopes,
And prostrate myself before a painted shrine,
Beating my hands upon the hot earth,
Quieting my eyes with the distant sparkle
Of the faint Spring sea.

I would recline upon a balcony
In purple curving folds of silk,
And my dress should be silvered with a pattern
Of butterflies and swallows,
And the black band of my obi
Should flash with gold, circular threads,
And glitter when I moved.
I would lean against the railing
While you sang to me of wars—

Past, and to come—
Sang and played the *samisen*.
Perhaps I would beat a little hand drum
In time to your singing;
Perhaps I would only watch the play of light
On the hilts of your two swords.

I would sit in a covered boat,
Rocking slowly to the narrow waves of a river,
While above us, an arc of moving lanterns,
Curved a bridge.
And beyond the bridge,
A hiss of gold
Blooming out of blackness,
Rockets exploded,
And died in a soft dripping of coloured stars.
We would float between the high trestles,
And drift away from the other boats,
Until the rockets flared without sound
And their falling stars hung silent in the sky
Like wistaria clusters above the ancient entrance of a temple.

I would anything
Rather than this cold paper,
With, outside, the quiet sun on the sides of burgeoning branches,
And inside, only my books.

At The Bookseller's

Hanging from the ceiling by threads
Are prints,
Hundreds of prints
Of actors and courtesans,
Cheap, everyday prints
To delight the common people.
Those which please the most are women
With long, slim fingers,
In dresses of snow-blue,
Of green the colour of the heart of a young onion,
Of rose, of black, of dead-leaf brown.
Over the dresses runs a light tracing
Of superimposed tissues:
Orange undulations, zigzag cinnabar trellises,
Patterns of purplish paulownias.
In the corner of one of the prints is written:
"Utamaro has here painted his elegant visage."
They cost nothing, these pictures,
They are only one of the cheap amusements of the populace,
Yet they say that the publisher: Tsoutaya,
Has made a fortune.

Violin Sonata by Vincent D'Indy

To Charles Martin Loeffler

A little brown room in a sea of fields,
Fields pink as rose-mallows
Under a fading rose-mallow sky.

Four candles on a tall iron candlestick,
Clustered like altar lights.
Above, the models of four brown Chinese junks
Sailing round the brown walls,
Silent and motionless.

The quick cut of a vibrating string,
Another, and another,
Biting into the silence.
Notes pierce, sharper and sharper;
They draw up in a freshness of sound,
Higher—higher, to the whiteness of intolerable beauty.
They are jagged and clear,
Like snow peaks against the sky;
They hurt like air too pure to breathe.
Is it catgut and horsehair,
Or flesh sawing against the cold blue gates of the sky?

The brown Chinese junks sail silently round the brown walls.

A cricket hurries across the bare floor.

The windows are black, for the sun has set.

Only the candles,
Clustered like altar lamps upon their tall candlestick,
Light the violinist as he plays.

WINTER'S TURNING

Snow is still on the ground,
But there is a golden brightness in the air.
Across the river,
Blue,
Blue,
Sweeping widely under the arches
Of many bridges,
Is a spire and a dome,
Clear as though ringed with ice-flakes,
Golden, and pink, and jocund.
On a near-by steeple,
A golden weather-cock flashes smartly,
His open beak "Cock-a-doodle-dooing"
Straight at the ear of Heaven.
A tall apartment house,
Crocus-coloured,
Thrusts up from the street
Like a new-sprung flower,
Another street is edged and patterned
With the bloom of bricks,
Houses and houses of rose-red bricks,
Every window a-glitter.
The city is a parterre,
Blowing and glowing,
Alight with the wind,
Washed over with gold and mercury.
Let us throw up our hats,
For we are past the age of balls
And have none handy.
Let us take hold of hands,
And race along the sidewalks,
And dodge the traffic in crowded streets.
Let us whir with the golden spoke-wheels
Of the sun.
For tomorrow Winter drops into the waste-basket,
And the calendar calls it March.

Eucharis Amazonica

Wax-white lilies
        shaped like narcissus,
Frozen snow-rockets
        burst from a thin green stem,
Your trumpets spray antennae
        like cold, sweet notes stabbing air.
In your cups
        is the sharpness of winds,
The white husks of your blooms
        crack as ice cracks,
You strike against the darkness
        as hoar-frost patterning a window.

Wax-white lilies,
Eucharis lilies,
Mary kissed your petals,
And the chill of pure snow
Burned her lips with its six-pointed seal.

AMY LOWELL

The Two Rains

Spring Rain

Tinkling of ankle bracelets.
Dull striking
Of jade and sardonyx
From whirling ends of jointed circlets.

Summer Rain

Clashing of bronze bucklers,
Screaming of horses.
Red plumes of head-trappings
Flashing above spears.

Good Gracious!

They say there is a fairy in every streak'd tulip.
I have rows and rows of them beside my door.
Hoop-la! Come out, Brownie,
And I will give you an emerald earring!
You had better come out,
For tomorrow may be stormy,
And I could never bring myself to part with my emerald earrings
Unless there was a moon.

Trees

The branches of the trees lie in layers
Above and behind each other,
And the sun strikes on the outstanding leaves
And turns them white,
And they dance like a splatter of pebbles
Against a green wall.

The trees make a solid path leading up in the air.
It looks as though I could walk upon it
If I only had courage to step out of the window.

Dawn Adventure

I stood in my window
      looking at the double cherry:
A great height of white stillness,
Underneath a sky
      the colour of milky grey jade.
Suddenly a crow flew between me and the tree—
Swooping, falling, in a shadow-black curve—
And blotted himself out in the blurred branches
      of a leafless ash.
There he stayed for sometime,
      and I could only distinguish him
      by his slight moving.
Then a wind caught the upper branches of the cherry,
And the long, white stems nodded up and down,
      casually, to me in the window,
Nodded—but overhead the grey jade clouds
      passed slowly, indifferently, toward the sea.

The Corner of Night and Morning

Crows are cawing over pine-trees,
They are teaching their young to fly
Above the tall pyramids of double cherries.
Rose lustre over black lacquer—
The feathers of the young birds reflect the rose rising sun.
Caw! Caw!
I want to go to sleep,
But perhaps it is better to stand in the window
And watch the crows teaching their young to fly
Over the pines and the pyramidal cherries,
In the rose-gold light
Of five o'clock on a May morning.

Beech, Pine, and Sunlight

The sudden April heat
Stretches itself
Under the smooth, leafless branches
Of the beech-tree,
And lies lightly
Upon the great patches
Of purple and white crocus
With their panting, wide-open cups.

A clear wind
Slips through the naked beech boughs,
And their shadows scarcely stir.
But the pine-trees beyond sigh
When it passes over them
And presses back their needles,
And slides gently down their stems.
It is a languor of pale, south-starting sunlight
Come upon a morning unawaked,
And holding her drowsing.

AMY LOWELL

Planning The Garden

Bring pencils, fine pointed,
For our writing must be infinitesimal;
And bring sheets of paper
To spread before us.
Now draw the plan of our garden beds,
And outline the borders and the paths
Correctly.
We will scatter little words
Upon the paper,
Like seeds about to be planted;
We will fill all the whiteness
With little words,
So that the brown earth
Shall never show between our flowers;
Instead, there will be petals and greenness
From April till November.
These narrow lines
Are rose-drifted thrift,
Edging the paths.
And here I plant nodding columbines,
With tree-tall wistarias behind them,
Each stem umbrella'd in its purple fringe.
Winged sweet-peas shall flutter next to pansies
All down the sunny centre.
Foxglove spears,
Thrust back against the swaying lilac leaves,
Will bloom and fade before the China asters
Smear their crude colours over Autumn hazes.
These double paths dividing make an angle
For bushes,
Bleeding hearts, I think,
Their flowers jigging
Like little ladies,
Satined, hoop-skirted,
Ready for a ball.
The round black circles

Mean striped and flaunting tulips,
The clustered trumpets of yellow jonquils,
And the sharp blue of hyacinths and squills.
These specks like dotted grain
Are coreopsis, bright as bandanas,
And ice-blue heliotrope with its sticky leaves,
And mignonette
Whose sober-coloured cones of bloom
Scent quiet mornings.
And poppies! Poppies! Poppies!
The hatchings shall all mean a tide of poppies,
Crinkled and frail and flowing in the breeze.

Wait just a moment,
Here's an empty space.
Now plant me lilies-of-the-valley—
This pear-tree over them will keep them cool
We'll have a lot of them
With white bells jingling.
The steps
Shall be all soft with stone-crop;
And at the top I'll make an arch of roses,
Crimson,
Bee-enticing.

There, it is done;
Seal up the paper.
Let us go to bed and dream of flowers.

AMY LOWELL

IMPRESSIONIST PICTURE OF A GARDEN

Give me sunlight, cupped in a paint brush,
And smear the red of peonies
Over my garden.
Splash blue upon it,
The hard blue of Canterbury bells,
Paling through larkspur
Into heliotrope,
To wash away among forget-me-nots.
Dip red again to mix a purple,
And lay on pointed flares of lilacs against bright green.
Streak yellow for nasturtiums and marsh marigolds
And flame it up to orange for my lilies.
Now dot it so—and so—along an edge
Of Iceland poppies.
Swirl it a bit, and faintly,
Now put a band of brutal, bleeding crimson
And tail it off to pink, to give the roses.
And while you're loaded up with pink,
Just blotch about that bed of phlox.
Fill up with cobalt and dash in a sky
As hot and heavy as you can make it;
Then tree-green pulled up into that
Gives a fine jolt of colour.
Strain it out,
And melt your twigs into the cobalt sky.
Toss on some Chinese white to flash the clouds,
And trust the sunlight you've got in your paint.
There is the picture.

A BATHER
After a Picture by Andreas Zorn

Thick dappled by circles of sunshine and fluttering shade,
Your bright, naked body advances, blown over by leaves,
Half-quenched in their various green, just a point of you showing,
A knee or a thigh, sudden glimpsed, then at once blotted into
The filmy and flickering forest, to start out again
Triumphant in smooth, supple roundness, edged sharp as white ivory,
Cool, perfect, with rose rarely tinting your lips and your breasts,
Swelling out from the green in the opulent curves of ripe fruit,
And hidden, like fruit, by the swift intermittence of leaves.
So, clinging to branches and moss, you advance on the ledges
Of rock which hang over the stream, with the wood smells about you,
The pungence of strawberry plants, and of gum-oozing spruces,
While below runs the water, impatient, impatient—to take you,
To splash you, to run down your sides, to sing you of deepness,
Of pools brown and golden, with brown-and-gold flags on their borders,
Of blue, lingering skies floating solemnly over your beauty,
Of undulant waters a-sway in the effort to hold you,
To keep you submerged and quiescent while over you glories
The Summer.
                    Oread, Dryad, or Naiad, or just
Woman, clad only in youth and in gallant perfection,
Standing up in a great burst of sunshine, you dazzle my eyes
Like a snow-star, a moon, your effulgence burns up in a halo,
For you are the chalice which holds all the races of men.

You slip into the pool and the water folds over your shoulder,
And over the tree-tops the clouds slowly follow your swimming,
And the scent of the woods is sweet on this hot Summer morning.

AMY LOWELL

Dog-Days

A ladder sticking up at the open window,
The top of an old ladder;
And all of Summer is there.

Great waves and tufts of wistaria surge across the window,
And a thin, belated blossom
Jerks up and down in the sunlight;
Purple translucence against the blue sky.
"Tie back this branch," I say,
But my hands are sticky with leaves,
And my nostrils widen to the smell of crushed green.
The ladder moves uneasily at the open window,
And I call to the man beneath,
"Tie back that branch."

There is a ladder leaning against the window-sill,
And a mutter of thunder in the air.

AUGUST
Late Afternoon

Smoke-colour, rose, saffron,
With a hard edge chipping the blue sky,
A great cloud hung over the village,
And the white-painted meeting-house,
And the steeple with the gilded weather-cock
Heading and flashing to the wind.

Hilly Country

Jangle of cow-bells through pine-trees.
Grasshoppers leaping up out of the grass.
The mountain is bloomed like a grape
(Silver, hazing over purple),
It blocks into the sky like a shadow.
The South wind blows intermittently,
And the clanking of the cow-bells comes up the hill in gusts.

Trees in Winter

PINE-TREES:
  Black clouds slowly swaying
  Over a white earth.

HEMLOCKS:
  Coned green shadows
  Through a falling veil.

ELM-TREES:
  Stiff black threads
  Lacing over silver.

CEDARS:
  Layered undulations
  Roofing naked ground.

ALMONDS:
  Flaring needles
  Stabbing at a grey sky.

WEEPING CHERRIES:
  Tossing smoke
  Swept down by wind.

OAKS:
  Twisted beams
  Cased in alabaster.

Sea Coal

Swift like the tongues of lilies,
Striped Amaryllis
Thrusting out of cloven basalt.
Amber and chalcedony,
And the snapping of sand
On rocks
Glazed by the wind.

Dolphins in Blue Water

Hey! Crackerjack—jump!
Blue water,
Pink water,
Swirl, flick, flitter;
Snout into a wave-trough,
Plunge, curl.
Bow over,
Under,
Razor-cut and tumble.
Roll, turn—
Straight—and shoot at the sky,
All rose-flame drippings.
Down ring,
Drop,
Nose under,
Hoop,
Tail,
Dive,
And gone;
With smooth over-swirlings of blue water,
Oil-smooth cobalt,
Slipping, liquid lapis lazuli,
Emerald shadings,
Tintings of pink and ochre.
Prismatic slidings
Underneath a windy sky.

AMY LOWELL

Motor Lights on A Hill Road

Yellow-green, yellow-green, yellow-green and silver,
Rimple of leaves,
Blowing,
Passing,
Flowing overhead,
Arched leaves,
Silver of twisted leaves;
Fan-like yellow glare
On tree-trunks.
Fluted side wake
Breaking from one polished stem to another.
Swift drop on a disappearing road,
Jolt—a wooden bridge,
And a flat sky opens in front.
Above—
The wide sky careers furiously past a still moon.
Suddenly—Slap!—green, yellow,
Leaves and no moon.
Ribbed leaves,
Chamfered light patterns
Playing on a pleaching of leaves.
Wind,
Strong, rushing,
Continuous, like the leaves.
Wind sliding beside us,
Meeting us,
Pointing against us through a yellow-green tunnel.
Dot. . . Dot. . . Dot. . .
Little square lights of windows,
Black walls stamping into silver mist,
Shingle roofs aflame like mica.
Elliptical cutting curve
Round a piazza where rocking-chairs creak emptily.
Square white fences
Chequer-boarding backwards.
Plunge at a black hill,

Flash into water-waving fluctuations.
Leaves gush out of the darkness
And boil past in yellow-green curds:
slip between them with the smoothness of oil.
Hooped yellow light spars
Banding green
Glide toward us,
Impinge upon our progress,
Open and let us through.
Liquid leaves lap the wheels,
Toss,
Splash,
Disappear.
Green and yellow water-slopes hang over us,
Close behind us,
Push us forward.
We are the centre of a green and yellow bubble,
Changing,
Expanding,
Skimming over the face of the world—
Green and yellow, occasionally tinged with silver.

AMY LOWELL

AS TOWARD ONE'S SELF

In a Time of Dearth

Before me,
On either side of me,
I see sand.
If I turn the corner of my house
I see sand.
Long—brown—
Lines and levels of flat
Sand.

If I could see a caravan Heave over the edge of it:
The camels wobbling and swaying,
Stepping like ostriches,
With rocking palanquins
Whose curtains conceal
Languors and faintnesses,

Muslins tossed aside,
And a disorder of cushions.
The swinging curtains would pique and solace me.
But I only see sand,
Long, brown sand,
Sand.

If I could see a herd of Arab horses
Galloping,
Their manes and tails pulled straight
By the speed of their going;
Their bodies sleek and round
Like bellying sails.
They would beat the sand with their fore-feet,
And scatter it with their hind-feet,
So that it whirled in a cloud of orange,
And the sun through it
Was clip-edged, without rays—and dun.
But I only see sand,

Long, brown, hot sand,
Sand.

If I could see a mirage
Blue-white at the horizon,
With palm-trees about it;
Tall, windless palm-trees, grouped about a glitter.
If I could strain towards it,
And think of the water creeping round my ankles,
Tickling under my knees,
Leeching up my sides,
Spreading over my back!
But I only feel the grinding beneath my feet.
And I only see sand,
Long, dry sand,
Scorching sand,
Sand.

If a sand-storm would come
And spit against my windows,
Snapping upon them, and ringing their vibrations;
Swirling over the roof,
Seeping under the door-jamb,
Suffocating me and making me struggle for air.
But I only see sand,
Sand lying dead in the sun,
Lines and lines of sand,
Sand.

I will paste newspapers over the windows to shut out the sand,
I will fit them into one another, and fasten the corners.
Then I will strike matches
And read of politics, and murders, and festivals,
Three years old.
But I shall not see the sand any more
And I can read
While my matches last.

AMY LOWELL

Aliens

The chatter of little people
Breaks on my purpose
Like the water-drops which slowly wear the rocks to powder.
And while I laugh
My spirit crumbles at their teasing touch.

MIDDLE AGE

Like black ice
Scrolled over with unintelligible patterns
                              by an ignorant skater
Is the dulled surface of my heart.

La Vie De Bohême

Alone, I whet my soul against the keen
Unwrinkled sky, with its long stretching blue.
I polish it with sunlight and pale dew,
And damascene it with young blowing leaves.
Into the handle of my life I set
Sprays of mignonette
And periwinkle,
Twisted into sheaves.
The colours laugh and twinkle.
Twined bands of roadways, liquid in the sheen
Of street lamps and the ruby shine of cabs,
Glisten for my delight all down its length;
And there are sudden sparks
Of morning ripplings over tree-fluttered pools.
My soul is fretted full of gleams and darks,
Pulsing and still.
Smooth-edged, untarnished, girded in my soul
I walk the world.

But in its narrow alleys,
The low-hung, dust-thick valleys
Where the mob shuffles its empty tread,
My soul is blunted against dullard wits,
Smeared with sick juices,
Nicked impotent for other than low uses.
Its arabesques and sparkling subtleties
Crusted to grey, and all its changing surfaces
Spread with unpalpitant monotonies.

I re-create myself upon the polished sky:
A honing-strop above converging roofs.
The patterns show again, like buried proofs
Of old, lost empires bursting on the eye
In hieroglyphed and graven splendour.

The whirling winds brush past my head,
And prodigal once more, a reckless spender
Of disregarded beauty, a defender
Of undesired faiths,
I walk the world.

Flame Apples

Little hot apples of fire,
Burst out of the flaming stem
Of my heart,
I do not understand how you quickened and grew,
And you amaze me
While I gather you.

I lay you, one by one,
Upon a table.
And now you seem beautiful and strange to me,
And I stand before you,
Wondering.

THE TRAVELLING BEAR

Grass-blades push up between the cobblestones
And catch the sun on their flat sides
Shooting it back,
Gold and emerald,
Into the eyes of passersby.

And over the cobblestones,
Square-footed and heavy,
Dances the trained bear.
The cobbles cut his feet,
And he has a ring in his nose
Which hurts him;
But still he dances,
For the keeper pricks him with a sharp stick,
Under his fur.

Now the crowd gapes and chuckles,
And boys and young women shuffle their feet in time to the dancing
    bear.
They see him wobbling
Against a dust of emerald and gold,
And they are greatly delighted.

The legs of the bear shake with fatigue,
And his back aches,
And the shining grass-blades dazzle and confuse him.
But still he dances,
Because of the little, pointed stick.

AMY LOWELL

MERCHANDISE

I made a song one morning,
Sitting in the shade under the hornbeam hedge.
I played it on my pipe,
And the clear notes delighted me,
And the little hedge-sparrows and the chipmunks
Also seemed pleased.
So I was very proud
That I had made so good a song.

Would you like to hear my song?
I will play it to you
As I did that evening to my Beloved,
Standing on the moon-bright cobbles
Underneath her window.
But you are not my Beloved,
You must give me a silver shilling,

Round and glittering like the moon.
Copper I will not take,
How should copper pay for a song
All made out of nothing,
And so beautiful!

The Poem

It is only a little twig
With a green bud at the end;
But if you plant it,
And water it,
And set it where the sun will be above it,
It will grow into a tall bush
With many flowers,
And leaves which thrust hither and thither
Sparkling.
From its roots will come freshness,
And beneath it the grass-blades
Will bend and recover themselves,
And clash one upon another
In the blowing wind.

But if you take my twig
And throw it into a closet
With mousetraps and blunted tools,
It will shrivel and waste.
And, some day,
When you open the door,
You will think it an old twisted nail,
And sweep it into the dust bin
With other rubbish.

AMY LOWELL

The Peddler of Flowers

I came from the country
With flowers,
Larkspur and roses,
Fretted lilies
In their leaves,
And long, cool lavender.

I carried them
From house to house,
And cried them
Down hot streets.
The sun fell
Upon my flowers,
And the dust of the streets
Blew over my basket.

That night
I slept upon the open seats
Of a circus,
Where all day long
People had watched
The antics
Of a painted clown.

Balls

Throw the blue ball above the little twigs of the
     tree-tops,
And cast the yellow ball straight at the buzzing stars.

All our life is a flinging of coloured balls
                to impossible distances.
And in the end what have we?
A tired arm—a tip-tilted nose.

Ah! Well! Give me the purple one.
Wouldn't it be a fine thing if I could make it stick
On top of the Methodist steeple?

AMY LOWELL

The Fanatic

Like Don Quixote, I tilted at a windmill.
On my good, grey horse I spurred at it,
Galloping heavily over the plain.
My lance pierced the framework of a sail and stuck there,
And the impact sent me sprawling on the ground.

My horse wandered away, cropping,
But I started up and fell upon the windmill,
With my dagger unsheathed.
Valiantly I stabbed a dipping sail,
But it rose before I could withdraw the weapon,
And the blade went up with it, gleaming—flickering.

Then I drew a pistol,
For I am an up-to-date knight
And my armory unrivalled.
I aimed above me,
At the sky between two sails.
Ping! went the bullet,
And a round, blue eye peeked at me through the wheeling sail.
I fired again—
Two eyes winked at me, jeering.

Then I ran at the windmill with my fists,
But it struck me down and left me.
All night I lay there,
And the great sails turned about and about,
And brushed me with their shadows,
For there was a moon.

FIREWORKS

You hate me and I hate you,
And we are so polite, we two!

But whenever I see you, I burst apart
And scatter the sky with my blazing heart.
It spits and sparkles in stars and balls,
Buds into roses -and flares, and falls.

Scarlet buttons, and pale green disks,
Silver spirals and asterisks,
Shoot and tremble in a mist
Peppered with mauve and amethyst.

I shine in the windows and light up the trees,
And all because I hate you, if you please.
And when you meet me, you rend asunder
And go up in a flaming wonder Of saffron cubes, and crimson moons,
And wheels all amaranths and maroons.

Golden lozenges and spades,
Arrows of malachites and jades,
Patens of copper, azure sheaves.
As you mount, you flash in the glossy leaves.

Such fireworks as we make, we two!
Because you hate me and I hate you.

AMY LOWELL

Trades

I want to be a carpenter,
To work all day long in clean wood,
Shaving it into little thin slivers
Which screw up into curls behind my plane;
Pounding square, black nails into white boards,
With the claws of my hammer glistening
Like the tongue of a snake.
I want to shingle a house,
Sitting on the ridge-pole in a bright breeze.
I want to put the shingles on neatly,
Taking great care that each is directly between two others.
I want my hands to have the tang of wood:
Spruce, Cedar, Cypress.
I want to draw a line on a board with a flat pencil,
And then saw along that line,
With the sweet-smelling sawdust piling up in a yellow heap at my feet.

That is the life!
Heigh-ho!
It is much easier than to write this poem.

GENERATIONS

You are like the stem
Of a young beech-tree,
Straight and swaying,
Breaking out in golden leaves.
Your walk is like the blowing of a beech-tree
On a hill.
Your voice is like leaves
Softly struck upon by a South wind.
Your shadow is no shadow, but a scattered sunshine;
And at night you pull the sky down to you
And hood yourself in stars.

But I am like a great oak under a cloudy sky,
Watching a stripling beech grow up at my feet.

Entente Cordiale

The young gentleman from the foreign nation
Sat on the sofa and smiled.
He stayed for two hours and I talked to him.
He answered agreeably,
He was very precise, very graceful, very enthusiastic.
I thought:
Is it possible that there are no nations, only individuals?
That it is the few who give gold and flowers,
While the many have only copper
So worn that even the stamp is obliterated?
I talked to the young gentleman from the foreign nation,
And the faint smell of copper assailed my nostrils:
Copper,
Twisted copper coins dropped by old women
Into the alms-boxes of venerable churches.

Castles in Spain

I build my poems with little strokes of ink
    Drawn shining down white paper, line and line,
    And there is nothing here which men call fine,
Nothing but hieroglyphs to make them think.
I have no broad and blowing plain to link
    And loop with aqueducts, no golden mine
    To crest my pillars, no bright twisted vine
Which I can train about a fountain's brink.
Those others laced their poems from sea to sea
    And floated navies over fields of grain,
      They fretted their full fancies in strong stone
    And struck them on the sky. And yet I gain;
For bombs and bullets cannot menace me,
      Who have no substance to be overthrown.
Cathedrals crash to rubbish, but my towers,
    Carved in the whirling and enduring brain,
Fade, and persist, and rise again, like flowers.

AMY LOWELL

PLUMMETS TO CIRCUMSTANCE

Ely Cathedral

Anzemic women, stupidly dressed and shod
In squeaky shoes, thump down the nave to laud an expurgated God.
Bunches of lights reflect upon the pavement where
The twenty benches stop, and through the close, smelled-over air
Gaunt arches push up their whited stones,
And cover the sparse worshippers with dead men's bones.
Behind his shambling choristers, with flattened feet
And red-flapped hood, the Bishop walks, complete
In old, frayed ceremonial. The organ wheezes
A mouldy psalm-tune, and a verger sneezes.
But the great Cathedral spears into the sky
Shouting for joy.

> What is the red-flapped Bishop praying for,
> by the by?

William Blake

He said he saw the spangled wings of angels
In a tree at Peckham Rye,
And Elija walking in the haying-fields;
So they beat him for his lies,
And 'prenticed him to an engraver.
Now his books sell for broad, round, golden guineas.
That's a bouncing turn of Fortune!
But we have the guineas,
Since our fathers were thrifty men
And knew the value of gold.

AMY LOWELL

An Incident

William Blake and Catherine Bourchier were
    married in the newly rebuilt Church of Battersea
    where the windows were beautifully painted to
    imitate real stained glass.
Pigments or crystal, what did it matter—when
    Jehovah sat on a cloud of curled fire over the doorway,
And angels with silver trumpets played Hosannas
    under the wooden groins of the peaked roof!
William and Catherine Blake left the painted windows
    behind in the newly rebuilt Church of Battersea,
But God and the angels went out with them;
And the angels played, on their trumpets under the plaster ceiling of
    their lodging,
Morning, and evening, and morning, forty-five round years.

Has the paint faded in the windows of Battersea Church, I wonder?

Peach-Colour to a Soap-Bubble

A man made a symphony
Out of the chords of his soul.
The notes ran upon the air like flights of chickadees,
They gathered together and hung
As bees above a syringa bush,
They crowded and clicked upon one another
In a flurry of progression,
And crashed in the simultaneous magnificence
Of a grand finale.
All this he heard,
But the neighbors heard only the croak
Of a wheezy, second-hand flageolet.

Forced to seek another lodging
He took refuge under the arch of a bridge,
For the river below him might be convenient
Some day.

Pyrotechnics

I

Our meeting was like the upward swish of a rocket
In the blue night.
I do not know when it burst;
But now I stand gaping,
In a glory of falling stars.

II

Hola! Hola! shouts the crowd, as the catharine-wheels sputter and turn.
Hola! They cheer the flower-pots and set pieces.
And nobody heeds the cries of a young man in shirt sleeves,
Who has burnt his fingers setting them off.

III

A King and Queen, and a couple of Generals,
Flame in coloured lights, Putting out the stars,
And making a great glare over the people wandering among the booths.
They are very beautiful and impressive,
And all the people say "Ah!"
By and by they begin to go out, Little by little.
The King's crown goes first,
Then his eyes,
Then his nose and chin.
The Queen goes out from the bottom up,
Until only the topmost jewel of her tiara is left.
Then that too goes;
And there is nothing but a frame of twisted wires,
With the stars twinkling through it.

The Bookshop

Pierrot had grown old.
He wore spectacles
And kept a shop.
Opium and hellebore
He sold
Between the covers of books,
And perfumes distilled from the veins of old ivory,
And poisons drawn from lotus seeds one hundred years withered
And thinned to the translucence of alabaster.
He sang a pale song of repeated cadenzas
In a voice cold as flutes
And shrill as desiccated violins.

I stood before the shop,
Fingering the comfortable vellum of an ancient volume,
Turning over its leaves,
And the dead moon looked over my shoulder
And fell with a green smoothness upon the page.
I read:
"I am the Lord thy God, thou shalt have none other gods but me."

Through the door came a chuckle of laughter
Like the tapping of unstrung kettledrums,
For Pierrot had ceased singing for a moment
To watch me reading.

Gargoyles
A Comedy of Oppositions

Thimble-rig on a village green,
Snake-charmers under a blue tent
Winding drugged sausage-bellies through thin arms.
Hiss
Of a yellow and magenta shawl
On a platform
Above trombones.

Tree lights
Drip cockatoos of colour
On broadest shoulders,
Dead eyes swim to a silver fish.
Gluttonous hands tear at apron strings,
Reach at the red side of an apple,
Slide under ice-floes,
And waltz clear through to the tropics
To sit among cocoanuts
And caress bulbous negresses with loquats in their hair.

A violin scorching on an F-sharp exit.
Stamp.
Stop.
Hayricks, and panting,
Noon roses guessed under calico—
A budded thorn-bush swinging
Against a smoke-dawn.
Hot pressing on sweet straw,
Laughs like whales floundering across air circles,
Wallows of smoothness,
Loose muscles dissolved upon lip-brushings,
Languid fluctuations,
Sleep oozing over wet flesh,
Cooling under the broad end of an angled shadow.
Absurd side-wiggle of geese before elephants;
A gold leopard snarls at a white-nosed donkey;

Panther-purrs rouse childhood to an edge of contortion;
Trumpets brawl beneath an oscillation of green balloons.

Why blow apple-blossoms into wind-dust?
Why drop a butterfly down the throat of a pig?
Timid shrinkings of a scarlet-runner bean
From pumpkin roughnesses.
Preposterous clamour of a cock for a tulip.
If your flesh is cold
Warm it on tea-pots
And let them be of Dresden china
With a coreopsis snarled in the handle.
Horse-bargainings do not become temples,
And sarabands are not danced on tea-trays of German silver.

Thin drums flatten the uprightness of distance,
A fading of drums shows lilac on the fallen beech leaves.
Emptiness of drums.
Nothing.

Burr of a rising moon.

To Winky

Cat,
Cat,
What are you?
Son, through a thousand generations, of the black leopards
Padding among the sprigs of young bamboo;
Descendant of many removals from the white panthers
Who crouch by night under the loquat-trees? You crouch under the
    orange begonias,
And your eyes are green
With the violence of murder,
Or half-closed and stealthy
Like your sheathed claws.
Slowly, slowly,
You rise and stretch
In a glossiness of beautiful curves,
Of muscles fluctuating under black, glazed hair.

Cat,
You are a strange creature.
You sit on your haunches
And yawn,
But when you leap
I can almost hear the whine
Of a released string,
And I look to see its flaccid shaking
In the place whence you sprang.

You carry your tail as a banner,
Slowly it passes my chair,
But when I look for you, you are on the table
Moving easily among the most delicate porcelains.
Your food is a matter of importance
And you are insistent on having
Your wants attended to,
And yet you will eat a bird and its feathers
Apparently without injury.

In the night, I hear you crying,
But if I try to find you
There are only the shadows of rhododendron leaves
Brushing the ground.
When you come in out of the rain,
All wet and with your tail full of burrs,
You fawn upon me in coils and subtleties;
But once you are dry
You leave me with a gesture of inconceivable impudence,
Conveyed by the vanishing quirk of your tail
As you slide through the open door.

You walk as a king scorning his subjects;
You flirt with me as a concubine in robes of silk.

Cat,
I am afraid of your poisonous beauty;
I have seen you torturing a mouse.
Yet when you lie purring in my lap
I forget everything but how soft you are,
And it is only when I feel your claws open upon my hand
That I remember
Remember a puma lying out on a branch above my head
Years ago.

Shall I choke you, Cat,
Or kiss you?
Really I do not know.

AMY LOWELL

Chopin

The cat and I
Together in the sultry night
Waited.
He greatly desired a mouse;
I, an idea.
Neither ambition was gratified.
So we watched
In a stiff and painful expectation.
Little breezes pattered among the trees,
And thin stars ticked at us
Faintly,
Exhausted pulses
Squeezing through mist.

Those others, I said!
And my mind rang hollow as I tapped it.
Winky, I said,
Do all other cats catch their mice?

* * *

It was low and long,
Ivory white, with doors and windows blotting blue upon it.
Wind choked in pomegranate-trees,
Rain rattled on lead roofs,
And stuttered along twisted conduit-pipes.
An eagle screamed out of the heavy sky,
And someone in the house screamed
"Ah, I knew that you were dead!"

So that was it:
Funeral chants,
And the icy cowls of buried monks;
Organs on iron midnights,
And long wax winding-sheets
Guttered from altar candles.

First this,
Then spitting blood.
Music quenched in blood,
Flights of arpeggios confused by blood,
Flute-showers of notes stung and arrested on a sharp chord,
Tangled in a web of blood.
"I cannot send you the manuscripts, as they are not yet finished.
I have been ill as a dog.
My illness has had a pernicious effect on the Preludes
Which you will receive God knows when."

* * *

He bore it. Therefore, Winky, drink some milk
And leave the mouse until tomorrow.
There are no blood-coloured pomegranate flowers
Hurling their petals in at the open window,
But you can sit in my lap
And blink at a bunch of cinnamon-eyed coreopsis
While I pull your ears
In the manner which you find so infinitely agreeable.

AMY LOWELL

Appuldurcombe Park

I am a woman, sick for passion,
Sitting under the golden beech-trees.
I am a woman, sick for passion,
Crumbling the beech leaves to powder in my fingers.
The servants say: "Yes, my Lady," and "No, my Lady."
And all day long my husband calls me
From his invalid chair:
"Mary, Mary, where are you, Mary? I want you."
Why does he want me?
When I come, he only pats my hand
And asks me to settle his cushions.
Poor little beech leaves,
Slowly falling,
Crumbling,
In the great park.
But there are many golden beech leaves
And I am alone.

I am a woman, sick for passion,
Walking between rows of painted tulips.
Parrot flowers, toucan-feathered flowers,
How bright you are!
You hurt me with your colours,
Your reds and yellows lance at me like flames.
Oh, I am sick—sick
And your darting loveliness hurts my heart.
You burn me with your parrot-tongues. Flame!
Flame!
My husband taps on the window with his stick:
"Mary, come in. I want you. You will take cold."

I am a woman, sick for passion,
Gazing at a white moon hanging over tall lilies.
The lilies sway and darken,
And a wind ruffles my hair.
There is a scrape of gravel behind me,

A red coat crashes scarlet against the lilies.
"Cousin-Captain!
I thought you were playing piquet with Sir Kenelm."
"Piquet, Dear Heart! And such a moon!"
Your red coat chokes me, Cousin-Captain.
Blood-colour, your coat:
I am sick—sick—for your heart.
Keep away from me, Cousin-Captain.
Your scarlet coat dazzles and confuses me.
O heart of red blood, what shall I do!
Even the lilies blow for the bee.
Does your heartbeat so loud, Beloved?
No, it is the tower-clock chiming eleven.
I must go in and give my husband his posset.
I hear him calling:
"Mary, where are you? I want you."

I am a woman, sick for passion,
Waiting in the long, black room for the funeral procession to pass.
I sent a messenger to town last night.
When will you come?
Under my black dress a rose is blooming.
A rose?- a heart?—it rustles for you with open petals.
Come quickly,
Dear,
For the corridors are full of noises.
In this fading light I hear whispers, And the steady, stealthy purr of
the wind.
What keeps you, Cousin-Captain? . . . What was that?
"Mary, I want you."
Nonsense, he is dead,
Buried by now.
Oh, I am sick of these long, cold corridors!
Sick—for what?
Why do you not come?

I am a woman, sick—sick -
Sick of the touch of cold paper,
Poisoned with the bitterness of ink.

Snowflakes hiss, and scratch the windows.
"Mary, where are you?"
That voice is like water in my ears;
I cannot empty them.
He wanted me, my husband,
But these stone parlours do not want me.
You do not want me either, Cousin-Captain.
Your coat lied,
Only your white sword spoke the truth.
"Mary! Mary!"
Will nothing stop the white snow
Sifting,
Sifting?
Will nothing stop that voice,
Drifting through the wide, dark halls?
The tower-clock strikes eleven dully, stifled with snow.
Softly over the still snow,
Softly over the lonely park,
Softly. . .
Yes, I have only my slippers, but I shall not take cold.
A little dish of posset.
Do the dead eat?
I have done it so long,
So strangely long.

THE BROKEN FOUNTAIN

Oblong, its jutted ends rounding into circles,
The old sunken basin lies with its flat, marble lip
An inch below the terrace tiles.
Over the stagnant water Slide reflections:
The blue-green of coned yews;
The purple and red of trailing fuchsias
Dripping out of marble urns;
Bright squares of sky
Ribbed by the wake of a swimming beetle.
Through the blue-bronze water
Wavers the pale uncertainty of a shadow.
An arm flashes through the reflections,
A breast is outlined with leaves.
Outstretched in the quiet water
The statue of a Goddess slumbers.
But when Autumn comes
The beech leaves cover her with a golden counterpane.

AMY LOWELL

The Dusty Hour-Glass

It had been a trim garden,
With parterres of fringed pinks and gillyflowers, and smooth-raked walks.
Silks and satins had brushed the box edges of its alleys.
The curved stone lips of its fishponds had held the rippled reflections
    of tricorns and powdered periwigs.
The branches of its trees had glittered with lanterns, and swayed to the
    music of flutes and violins.

Now, the fishponds are green with scum;
The paths and flower-beds are run together and overgrown.
Only at one end is an octagonal Summer-house not yet in ruins.
Through the lozenged panes of its windows, you can see the interior:
A dusty bench; a fireplace
        with a lacing of letters carved in the stone above it;

A broken ball of worsted
        rolled away into a corner.

Dolci, dolci, i giorni passata!

THE FLUTE

"Stop! What are you doing?"
"Playing on an old flute."
"That's Heine's flute—you mustn't touch it."
"Why not, if I can make it sound."
"I don't know why not, but you mustn't."
"I don't believe I can—much. It's full of dust.

    Still, listen:

The rose moon whitens the lifting leaves.
Heigh-o! The nightingale sings!
Through boughs and branches the moon-thread weaves.

Ancient as time are these midnight things.

The nightingale's notes over-bubble the night.
Heigh-o! Yet the night is so big
He stands on his nest in a wafer of light,
And the nest was once a philosopher's wig.

Moon-sharp needles, and dew on the grass.
Heigh-o! It flickers, the breeze!
Kings, philosophers, periwigs pass;
Nightingale eggs hatch under the trees.

Wigs, and pigs, and kings, and courts.
Heigh-o! Rain on the flower!
The old moon thinks her white, bright thoughts,
And trundles away before the shower.

"Well, you got it to play."
"Yes, a little. And it has lovely silver mountings."

AMY LOWELL

FLOTSAM

She sat in a Chinese wicker chair
Wide at the top like a spread peacock's tail,
And toyed with a young man's heart which she held lightly in her fingers.
She tapped it gently,
Held it up to the sun and looked through it,
Strung it on a chain of seed-pearls and fastened it about her neck,
Tossed it into the air and caught it,
Deftly, as though it were a ball.
Before her on the grass sat the young man.
Sometimes he felt an ache where his heart had been,
But he brushed it aside.
He was intent on gazing, and had no time for anything else.
Presently she grew tired and handed him back his heart,
But he only laid it on the ground beside him
And went on gazing.

When the maidservant came to tidy up,
     She found the heart on the grass.
"What a pretty thing," said the maidservant,
"It is red as a ruby!"
So she picked it up,
And carried it into the house,
And ran a ribbon through it,
And hung it on the looking-glass in her bedroom.
There it hung for many days,
Banging back and forth as the wind blew it.

LITTLE IVORY FIGURES PULLED WITH STRING

Is it the tinkling of mandolins which disturbs you?
Or the dropping of bitter-orange petals among the coffee-cups?
Or the slow creeping of the moonlight between the olive-trees?

> *Drop! Drop! the rain*
> *Upon the thin plates of my heart.*

String your blood to chord with this music,
Stir your heels upon the cobbles to the rhythm of a dance-tune.
They have slim thighs and arms of silver;
The moon washes away their garments;
They make a pattern of fleeing feet in the branch shadows,
And the green grapes knotted about them
Burst as they press against one another.

> *The rain knocks upon the plates of my heart,*
> *They are crumpled with its beating.*

Would you drink only from your brains, Old Man?
See, the moonlight has reached your knees,
It falls upon your head in an accolade of silver.
Rise up on the music,
Fling against the moon-drifts in a whorl of young light bodies:
Leaping grape-clusters,
Vine leaves tearing from a grey wall.
You shall run, laughing, in a braid of women,
And weave flowers with the frosty spines of thorns.
Why do you gaze into your glass,
And jar the spoons with your finger-tapping?

> *The rain is rigid on the plates of my heart.*
> *The murmur of it is loud—loud.*

AMY LOWELL

ON THE MANTELPIECE

A thousand years went to her making,
A thousand years of experiments in pastes and glazes. But now she stands
In all the glory of the finest porcelain and the most delicate paint,
A Dresden china shepherdess,
Flaunted before a tall mirror
On a high mantelpiece.

"Beautiful shepherdess,
I love the little pink rosettes on your shoes,
The angle of your hat sets my heart a-singing.
Drop me the purple rose you carry in your hand
That I may cherish it,
And that, at my death,
Which I feel is not far off,
It may lie upon my bier."

So the shepherdess threw the purple rose over the mantelpiece,
But it splintered in fragments on the hearth.

Then from below there came a sound of weeping,
And the shepherdess beat her hands
And cried:
"My purple rose is broken,
It was the flower of my heart."
And she jumped off the mantelpiece
And was instantly shattered into seven hundred and twenty pieces.
But the little brown cricket who sang so sweetly
Scuttled away into a crevice of the marble
And went on warming his toes and chirping.

AS TOWARD WAR

Misericordia

He earned his bread by making wooden soldiers,
With beautiful golden instruments,
Riding dapple-grey horses.
But when he heard the fanfare of trumpets
And the long rattle of drums
As the army marched out of the city,
He took all his soldiers
And burned them in the grate;
And that night he fashioned a ballet-dancer
Out of tinted tissue-paper,
And the next day he started to carve a Pieta
On the steel hilt
Of a cavalry sword.

DREAMS IN WAR TIME

I

I wandered through a house of many rooms.
It grew darker and darker,
Until, at last, I could only find my way
By passing my fingers along the wall.
Suddenly my hand shot through an open window,
And the thorn of a rose I could not see
Pricked it so sharply
That I cried aloud.

II

I dug a grave under an oak-tree.
With infinite care,
I stamped my spade.
Into the heavy grass.
The sod sucked it,
And I drew it out with effort,
Watching the steel run liquid in the moonlight
As it came clear.
I stooped, and dug, and never turned,
For behind me,
On the dried leaves,
My own face lay like a white pebble,
Waiting.

III

I gambled with a silver money.
The dried seed-vessels of "honesty"
Were stacked in front of me.
Dry, white years slipping through my fingers
One by one.
One by one, gathered by the Croupier.
"Faites vos jeux, Messieurs."

AMY LOWELL

I staked on the red,
And the black won.
Dry years,
Dead years;
But I had a system,
I always staked on the red.

IV

I painted the leaves of bushes red
And shouted: "Fire! Fire!" But the neighbors only laughed.
"We cannot warm our hands at them," they said.
Then they cut down my bushes,
And made a bonfire,
And danced about it.
But I covered my face and wept,
For ashes are not beautiful
Even in the dawn.

V

I followed a procession of singing girls
Who danced to the glitter of tambourines.
Where the street turned at a lighted corner,
I caught the purple dress of one of the dancers,
But, as I grasped it, it tore,
And the purple dye ran from it
Like blood
Upon the ground.

VI

I wished to post a letter,
But although I paid much,
Still the letter was overweight.
"What is in this package?" said the clerk,
"It is very heavy."
"Yes," I said,
"And yet it is only a dried fruit."

VII

I had made a kite,
On it I had pasted golden stars
And white torches,
And the tail was spotted scarlet like a tiger-lily,
And very long. I flew my kite,
And my soul was contented
Watching it flash against the concave of the sky.
My friends pointed at the clouds;
They begged me to take in my kite.
But I was happy
Seeing the mirror shock of it
Against the black clouds.
Then the lightning came
And struck the kite.
It puffed—blazed—fell.
But still I walked on,
In the drowning rain,
Slowly winding up the string.

Spectacles

He was a landscape architect.

All day he planned Dutch gardens: rectangular,
    squared with tulips; Italian gardens: dark with myrtle, thick with
    running water; English gardens: prim, box-edged, espaliered
    fruit trees flickering on walls, borders of snap-dragons, pansies,
    marjoram, rue.

On Saturday afternoons, he did not walk into the country.
    He paid a quarter and went to a cinema show, and gazed—gazed—
    at marching soldiers, at guns firing and recoiling, at waste grounds
    strewn with mutilated dead. When he took off his glasses, there
    was moisture upon them, and his eyes hurt. He could not see to
    use a periscope, they said, yet he could draw gardens.

His firm dismissed him for designing a military garden:
    forts, and redoubts, and salients, in hemlock and yew, and a puzzle
    of ditches, damp, deep, floored with forget-me-nots. It was a
    wonderful thing, but quite mad, of course.

When they took his body from the river, the eyes were wide open,
    and the lids were so stiffened that they buried him without closing
    them.

In the Stadium
Marshal Joffre Reviewing The Harvard Regiment, May 12, 1917

A little old man Huddled up in a corner of a carriage,
Rapidly driven in front of throngs of people
With his hand held to a perpetual salute.
The people cheer,
But he has heard so much cheering.
On his breast is a row of decorations.
He feels his body recoil before attacks of pain.

They are all like this:
Napoleon,
Hannibal,
Great Caesar even,
But that he died out of time.
Sick old men,
Driving rapidly before a concourse of people,
Gay with decorations,
Crumpled with pain.

The drum-major lifts his silver-headed stick,
And the silver trumpets and tubas,
The great round drums,
Each with an H on them,
Crash out martial music.
Heavily rhythmed march music
For the stepping of a regiment.

Slant lines of rifles,
A twinkle of stepping,
The regiment comes.
The young regiment,
Boys in khaki
With slanted rifles.

The young bodies of boys
Bulwarked in front of us.

AMY LOWELL

The white bodies of young men
Heaped like sandbags
Against the German guns.

This is war:
Boys flung into a breach
Like shovelled earth;
And old men,
Broken,
Driving rapidly before crowds of people
In a glitter of silly decorations.

Behind the boys
And the old men,
Life weeps,
And shreds her garments
To the blowing winds.

AFTER WRITING "THE BRONZE HORSES"

I am so tired.
I have run across the ages with spiritless feet,
I have tracked man where he falls splintered in defeat,
I have watched him shoot up like green sprouts at dawning,
I have seen him blossom, and fruit, and offer himself, fawning,
On golden platters to kings.
I have seen him reel with drunk blood,
I have followed him in flood
Sweep over his other selves.
I have written things
Which sucked the breath
Out of my lungs, and hung
My heart up in a frozen death.
I have picked desires
Out of purple fires
And set them on the shelves
Of my mind,
Nonchalantly,
As though my kind
Were unlike these.
But while I did this, my bowels contracted in twists of fear.
I felt myself squeeze
Myself dry,
And wished that I could shrivel before Destiny
Could snatch me back into the vortex of Yesterday.
Wheels and wheels -
And only your hand is firm.
The very paths of my garden squirm
Like snakes between the brittle flowers,
And the sunrise gun cuts off the hours
Of this day and the next.
The long, dusty volumes are the first lines of a text.
Oh, Beloved, must we read?
Must you and I, alone in the midst of trees,
See their green alleys printing with the screed
Which counts these new men, these

Terrible resurrections of old wars.
I wish I had not seen so much:
The roses that you wear are bloody scars,
And you the moon above a battle-field;
So all my thoughts are grown to such.
A body peeled
Down to a skeleton,
A grinning jaw-bone in a bed of mignonette.
What good is it to say "Not yet."
I tell you I am tired
And afraid.

THE FORT

The disappearing guns
Are hidden in their concrete emplacements,
But, above them,
Meadow grasses fall and recover,
Bend and stiffen,
Go dark, burn light,
In the play of a gusty wind.
A black-and-orange butterfly
Flits about among the butter-and-egg flowers,
And the sea stands up,
Tall in perspective,
With full-spread schooners
Sprinkled upon it
As roses are powdered
Over a ribbon of moiré blue.

The disappearing guns are black
In grey concrete emplacements
With here and there a touch of red rust.

Wind cuts through the grasses,
Rasps upon them,
Draws a bow note out along them.
Swish!—Oh-h-h!
And the low waves
Crash soft constant cymbals
On the shingle beach
At the foot of the cliff.
Good Gracious!
A seal!
After how many years?
He turns his head to look at us,
He lolls on his rock contented and hot with sun.

The disappearing guns would shoot over him
If they were to fire.

AMY LOWELL

Is he held in the harbour
By the submarine nets, I wonder?

"You turn the crank so.
Do you see her move?
If you stand here, you can see the springs for the recoil."
Perhaps I can,
But I cannot see the orange butterfly,
Nor the seal,
Nor the little ships
Drawn across the tall, streaked sea.
And all I can hear
Is the jingle of a piano
In the men's quarters
Playing a comic opera tune.
Is it possible that, at night,
The little flitter-bats
Hang under the lever-wheels of the disappearing guns
In their low emplacements
To escape from the glare
Of the search-lights,
Shooting over the grasses
To the sea?

Camouflaged Troop-ship
Boston Harbour

Uprightness,
Masts, one behind another,
Syncopated beyond and between one another,
Clouding together,
Becoming confused.
A mist of grey, blurring stems Platformed upon horizontal thicknesses.
Decks,
Bows and sterns escaping fore and aft,
A long line of flatness
Darker than the fog of masts,
More solid,
Monotonous grey.
Dull smokestacks
Plotting lustreless clouds.
An ebb-tide
Slowly sucking the refuse of a harbour
Seaward.

The ferry turns;
And there,
On the starboard quarter,
Thrust out from the vapour-wall of ships:
Colour.
Against the perpendicular:
Obliqueness.
In front of the horizontal:
A crenelated edge.
A vessel, grooved and conical, Shell-shaped, flower-flowing,
Gothic, bizarre, and unrelated.
Black spirals over cream-colour Broken at a half-way point.
A slab of black amidships.

At the stern,
Lines:

Rising from the water,
Curled round and over,
Whorled, scattered,
Drawn upon one another.
Snakes starting from a still ocean,
Writhing over cream-colour,
Crashed upon and cut down
By a flat, impinging horizon.

The sea is grey and low,
But the vessel is high with upthrusting lines:
Hair lines incessantly moving,
Broad bands of black turning evenly over emptiness,
Intorting upon their circuits,
Teasing the eye with indefinite motion,
Coming from nothing,
Ending without cessation.

Drowned hair drifting against mother-of-pearl;
Kelp-aprons
Shredded upon a yellow beach;
Black spray
Salted over cream-grey wave-tops.

You hollow into rising water,
You double-turn under the dripped edges of clouds,
You move in a hundred directions,
And keep to a course the eye cannot see.
Your terrible lines
Are swift as the plunge of a kingfisher;
They vanish as one traces them,
They are constantly vanishing,
And yet you swing at anchor in the grey harbour
Waiting for your quota of troops.
Men will sail in you,
Netted in whirling paint,
Held like brittle eggs
In an osier basket.

They will sail,
Over black-skinned water,
Into a distance of cream-colour and vague shadow-shotted blue.

The ferry whistle blows for the landing.
Start the engine
That we may not block
The string of waiting carts.

AMY LOWELL

September, 1918

This afternoon was the colour of water falling through sunlight;
The trees glittered with the tumbling of leaves;
The sidewalks shone like alleys of dropped maple leaves,
And the houses ran along them laughing out of square, open windows.
Under a tree in the park,
Two little boys, lying flat on their faces,
Were carefully gathering red berries
To put in a pasteboard box.

Some day there will be no war,
Then I shall take out this afternoon
And turn it in my fingers,
And remark the sweet taste of it upon my palate,
And note the crisp variety of its flights of leaves.
Today I can only gather it
And put it into my lunch-box,
For I have time for nothing
But the endeavour to balance myself
Upon a broken world.

THE NIGHT BEFORE THE PARADE
April 25, 1919

Birds are calling through the rain,
Glass bells dropping across the patter of falling rain.
The garden soaks, and breathes, and lifts up the spear-green leaves of
    tulips
And the long, golden mouths of daffodils
To the downpour, And the high blossoms of forsythia
Tremble vaguely, and bend to let the rain run off them
And spill over the little red peony fronds
Uncurling at their feet.
It is wet, and cool, and pleasant.
Why should words rattle upon this quietness?
    "Adders writhe from the sunken eyes
    Of statues, in Persepolis."

Clashes of bells bursting in a grey sky,
And a clock striking jubilees of brass hours, one after another.
Gas-jets flicker, and spin sudden lights across the battle-flags draped
    to the pillars.
The church sighs in the evening rain,
Kneeling beneath the dim clouds in a stillness of adoration.
Beauty of stone, of glass, of memories,
Worshipful beauty spotted by the snarl of words—
    "Adders writhe from the sunken eyes
    Of statues, in Persepolis."

They have put up stands,
Flimsy wooden stands to crush out the little green life of the grass.
Tomorrow the crowds will cheer,
And the streets will shine with flags and gilding.
The people will shout themselves hoarse
When the green helmets and the white bayonets
Sweep along the streets.
Only the little grass-blades will cry and languish,
Weeping: "We are the cousins of the grasses of France,
The kind grasses who cover the graves of those you have forgotten."

AMY LOWELL

Then they will hiss under the cruel stands,
And the words will run, and glare, and brighten:
> "Adders writhe from the sunken eyes
> Of statues, in Persepolis."

Rain on a roofless city,
Rain over broken walls and towers scattered to a ring of ruins,
Pale splendours of hard stone melted to the purple bloom of orchises,
And poppies thrust between the basalt paving-blocks of roads leading
    to a waste of blue-tongued thistles.
Where did I see this?
Not in the leafless branches of the ash-tree,
Not in the glitter of my wet window-sill,
Not in the smooth garden filling itself with good rain.
There are fireworks tonight,
The first for two years.
And listen to the rain!
Listen—listen—
Prayers, and flowers, and a booming of guns.
It blurs—
Do I hear anything?
What are you reading?
> "Adders writhe from the sunken eyes
> Of statues, in Persepolis."

AS TOWARD IMMORTALITY

ON A CERTAIN CRITIC

Well, John Keats,
I know how you felt when you swung out of the inn
And started up Box Hill after the moon.
Lord! How she twinkled in and out of the box bushes
Where they arched over the path.
How she peeked at you and tempted you,
And how you longed for the "naked waist" of her
You had put into your second canto.
You felt her silver running all over you,
And the shine of her flashed in your eyes
So that you stumbled over roots and things.
Ah! How beautiful! How beautiful!
Lying out on the open hill
With her white radiance touching you
Lightly,
Flecking over you.
"My Lady of the Moon, I flow out to your whiteness, Brightness.
    My hands cup themselves
About your disk of pearl and fire;
Lie upon my face,
Burn me with the cold of your hot white flame.
Diana,
High, distant Goddess,
I kiss the needles of this furze bush
Because your feet have trodden it.
Moon!
Moon!
I am prone before you.
Pity me,
And drench me in loveliness.
I have written you a poem
I have made a girdle for you of words;
Like a shawl my words will cover you,
So that men may read of you and not be burnt as I have been.
Sere my heart until it is a crinkled leaf,
I have held you in it for a moment,
And exchanged my love with yours,

On a high hill at midnight.
Was that your tear or mine, Bright Moon?
It was round and full of moonlight.
Don't go!
My God! Don't go!
You escape from me,
You slide through my hands.
Great Immortal Goddess,
Dearly Beloved,
Don't leave me.
My hands clutch at moonbeams,
And catch each other.
My Dear! My Dear!
My beautiful far-shining lady!
Oh! God!
I am tortured with this anguish of unbearable beauty."

Then you stumbled down the hill, John Keats,
Perhaps you fell once or twice;
It is a rough path,
And you weren't thinking of that.
Then you wrote,
By a wavering candle,
And the moon frosted your window till it looked like a sheet of blue ice.
And as you tumbled into bed, you said:
"It's a piece of luck I thought of coming out to Box Hill."

Now comes a sprig little gentleman,
And turns over your manuscript with his mincing fingers,
And tabulates places and dates.
He says your moon was a copy-book maxim,
And talks about the spirit of solitude,
And the salvation of genius through the social order.
I wish you were here to damn him
With a good, round, agreeable oath, John Keats,
But just snap your fingers,
You and the moon will still love,
When he and his papers have slithered away
In the bodies of innumerable worms.

A Note About the Author

Amy Lowell (1874–1925) was an American poet. Born into an elite family of businessmen, politicians, and intellectuals, Lowell was a member of the so-called Boston Brahmin class. She excelled in school from a young age and developed a habit for reading and book collecting. Denied the opportunity to attend college by her family, Lowell traveled extensively in her twenties and turned to poetry in 1902. While in England with her lover Ada Dwyer Russell, she met American poet Ezra Pound, whose influence as an imagist and fierce critic of Lowell's work would prove essential to her poetry. In 1912, only two years after publishing her first poem in *The Atlantic Monthly*, Lowell produced *A Dome of Many-Coloured Glasses,* her debut volume of poems. In addition to such collections of her own poems as *Sword Blades and Poppy Seed* (1914) and *Men, Women, and Ghosts* (1916), Lowell published translations of 8th century Chinese poet Li Tai-po and, at the time of her death, had been working on a biography of English Romantic John Keats.

A Note from the Publisher

bookfinity™

Discover more of your favorite classics with Bookfinity™.

- Track your reading with custom book lists.
- Get great book recommendations for your personalized Reader Type.
- Add reviews for your favorite books.
- AND MUCH MORE!

Visit **bookfinity.com** and take the fun Reader Type quiz to get started.

Enjoy our classic and modern companion pairings!

Printed in the USA
CPSIA information can be obtained
at www.ICGtesting.com
JSHW021513220124
55857JS00001B/9

9 798888 970041